English

The 11+
10-Minute Tests

For GL & other test providers

Book 2

Ages
10-11

Practise • Prepare • Pass
Everything your child needs for 11+ success

How to use this book

This book is made up of 10-minute tests and puzzle pages.
There are answers and detailed explanations in the pull-out section at the back of the book.

10-Minute Tests

- There are 33 tests in this book, consisting of 17 comprehension tests worth 9 marks each, and 16 proofreading tests worth 18 marks each. Each test is a bite-sized version of a full-length 11+ test, focusing on either the comprehension part or the proofreading part of the test.

- Each test is designed to cover a good range of the question styles and topics that your child could come across in their 11+ test, at the same difficulty level.

- Your child should aim to score at least 8 out of 9 in each comprehension test and 16 out of 18 in each proofreading test. If they score less than this, use their results to work out the areas they need more practice on.

- If your child hasn't managed to finish the test in time, they need to work on increasing their speed, whereas if they have made a lot of mistakes, they need to work more carefully.

- Keep track of your child's scores using the progress chart on the inside back cover of the book.

Puzzle Pages

- There are 10 puzzle pages in this book, which are a great break from test-style questions. They encourage children to practise the same skills that they will need in the test, but in a fun way.

Published by CGP

Editors:
Marc Barnard, Zoe Fenwick, Sophie Herring, Holly Robinson, James Summersgill, Jack Tooth and Sean Walsh.

With thanks to Alison Griffin and Glenn Rogers for the proofreading.
With thanks to Jan Greenway for the copyright research.

ISBN: 978 1 78294 768 4
Printed by Elanders Ltd, Newcastle upon Tyne
Clipart from Corel®

Based on the classic CGP style created by Richard Parsons.

Contents

You have **10 minutes** to do this test. Work as quickly and accurately as you can.

Read this passage carefully and answer the questions that follow.

Vikings in America

It is popularly thought that the first European to visit America was Christopher Columbus in 1492, but that is not true. Archaeological evidence shows that Viking explorers had reached the coast of mainland North America as early as AD 985.

According to the Icelandic sagas — a series of texts recounting the history of
5   Iceland — Vikings reached Greenland, off the coast of North America, in the 980s. Erik the Red, a Norse* explorer, had been banished from Iceland for manslaughter* and made passage to an icy land to the northwest of Iceland. Despite its frosty climate, Erik called the island 'Greenland' because he wanted to give other Norseman the impression that it was a green and fertile land. Around the year AD
10 1000, ships arrived from Iceland and established the first Norse towns in Greenland.

A few years after Greenland was colonised, Erik the Red's son, Leif Erikson, went on a voyage to explore the islands to the west of Greenland. He came across an area he called 'Vinland' (probably the Canadian island of Newfoundland) where he established a camp.

15 During the next few years, there were a few more expeditions to Vinland and some examples of peaceful trade been the Vikings and Native Americans, or 'Skraelings' as the Vikings called them. But according to the sagas, when the Viking camp was attacked by Skraelings with catapults, all of the Viking men fled. Leif's sister, Freydis Eiriksdottir, was eight months pregnant and unable to keep up with the
20 fleeing men. She proclaimed that she could fight better than them and picked up a sword that had been dropped. She struck the sword against her chest and let out a ferocious battle cry. The Skraelings were so petrified that they retreated.

However, the settlement in Vinland did not last long and was mysteriously abandoned. Norse settlement in Greenland lasted until the 15th century. Historians
25 have debated as to why the Norsemen left — some believe the Norse settlers got bored with the island, others believe a plague or fierce winters drove them out.

* Norse — *someone from Scandinavia, a Viking*
*manslaughter — *accidental murder*

2

1. How do we know Vikings explored North America?

    _____

2. Give another word or phrase that means the same as
    "recounting" (line 4) as it is used in the text.

    _____

3. Explain in your own words why Erik the Red left Iceland.

    _____

    _____

4. According to the text, why did Erik the Red name the island 'Greenland'?
    Tick the box next to the correct answer.

    A   It was a green and fertile land.   ☐

    B   He wanted to attract settlers there.   ☐

    C   The surrounding sea was green.   ☐

    D   He planned to grow crops there.   ☐

5. Which of the following statements about Erik the Red is false?
    Tick the box next to the correct answer.

    A   Erik the Red was European.   ☐

    B   Erik the Red probably left Greenland in the 15th century.   ☐

    C   Erik the Red appears in the Icelandic sagas.   ☐

    D   Erik the Red had at least two children.   ☐

TURN OVER ➡

6. Find a word from the text that means the same as 'announced'.

    _____

7. "the settlement in Vinland did not last long" (line 23). Which of the following
    words is an adverb? Tick the box next to the correct answer.

    A   settlement   ☐

    B   in   ☐

    C   last   ☐

    D   long   ☐

8. Which of the following statements is true?
    Tick the box next to the correct answer.

    A   The Vikings never left Greenland.   ☐

    B   Vinland was inhabited for longer than Greenland.   ☐

    C   Greenland was inhabited for longer than Vinland.   ☐

    D   Columbus visited Vinland in 1492.   ☐

9. Why did the Vikings leave Vinland? Tick the box next to the correct answer.

    A   Attacks by the Skraelings forced them to leave.   ☐

    B   The weather became too cold.   ☐

    C   The settlers were wiped out by disease.   ☐

    D   It is not clear from the text.   ☐

END OF TEST

/ 9

You have **10 minutes** to do this test. Work as quickly and accurately as you can.

> This passage contains some spelling mistakes.
> Write the passage out again with the correct spellings.

1. "I really apreciate your assistance, Sandra," Nick said, looking at the enourmous buffet that she had organised in the lesure centre to celabrate his daughter's birthday. Sandra was deturmined to throw a memorable party.

    _____

    _____

    _____

    _____

> This passage has some punctuation mistakes.
> Write the passage out again with the correct punctuation.

2. Saif was sad to say "goodbye to his friend's. Although he was only going away for six months it felt like an eternity. After giving them a hug Ron, Saif's brother drove him to the airport.

    _____

    _____

    _____

TURN OVER ➡

Test 2

For each numbered line, choose the word which completes the passage correctly. The passage needs to make sense and be written in correct English. Circle the correct letter.

3. Mrs Jones was the **frighten** **scaring** **frighteningest** **scares** **scariest** teacher in
   A · · · · · · · · B · · · · · · · · · · · · C · · · · · · · · · · D · · · · · · · E

4. school. Classes would **falls** **fallen** **fall** **coming** **comes** silent if they heard her
   · · · · · · · · · · · · · · · · · A · · · · · · · B · · · · · · C · · · · · · D · · · · · · · E

5. heels hit the floor of the corridor outside. **While** **What** **When** **Whereas** **Where**
   · A · · · · · · B · · · · · · C · · · · · · · D · · · · · · · E

6. she entered the classroom, you **should** **could** **can** **ought** **will** smell the fear.
   · A · · · · · · · · B · · · · · C · · · · · · D · · · · · E

7. She would then choose someone, seemingly **at** **in** **of** **if** **with** random, to send
   · A · · B · · C · · D · · · E

8. out and **shouted** **spoke** **shouts** **shout** **speaks** at in the corridor. Everyone
   · · · · · · · · · · · · A · · · · · · · · · B · · · · · · · · C · · · · · · · · D · · · · · · · · E

9. prayed it wouldn't be them. Once, I foolishly **leaved** **left** **leave** **leaves** **leaving**
   · A · · · · · · · B · · · · · · · C · · · · · · · · D · · · · · · · · E

10. my homework on the bus. I **sitting** **sit** **sits** **sitted** **sat** trembling in my seat,
    · A · · · · · · · B · · · · C · · · · · D · · · · · E

terrified of what she would say.

END OF TEST

/ 18

You have **10 minutes** to do this test. Work as quickly and accurately as you can.

Read this passage carefully and answer the questions that follow.

An adapted extract from 'Mary Barton'

"Where are the fire engines?" Margaret asked her neighbour.

"They're coming, no doubt; but it's hardly been ten minutes since we first found out about the fire. It is raging quickly through the mill with this wind."

"Has no one gone for a ladder?" gasped Mary, as the men in the mill were visibly,
5 though not audibly, begging the huge crowd below for help.

"Aye, Wilson's son and another man were off like a shot, well-nigh five minutes ago." Wilson then, was the man whose figure she could see against the ever increasing dull hot light behind, whenever the smoke was clear. That was George Wilson? Mary sickened with terror. She knew he worked for Carsons' mill; but at
10 first she had had no idea any lives were in danger. Since she had become aware of this, the heated air, the roaring flames, the dizzy light, and the agitated and murmuring crowd had bewildered her thoughts.

"Oh! Let us go home, Margaret; I cannot stay."

"We cannot go! See how we are wedged in by folks. Poor Mary! You won't
15 hanker after a fire again. Stop! Listen!"

Through the hushed crowd they could hear the rattle of the fire engine and the heavy, quick tread of loaded horses.

"Thank God!" said Margaret's neighbour, "the engine's come."

Another pause; the fire hydrants were stiff, and water could not be got.
20 Then there was a pressure through the crowd, the front rows bearing back on those behind, until the girls were sick with the close confinement.

Elizabeth Gaskell

TURN OVER ➡

Answer these questions about the text. You can refer back to the text if you need to.

1. Why is the fire in the mill spreading rapidly?

   _____

2. Lines 4-5 state that the men in the mill were "visibly, though not audibly" begging for help. What does this mean? Tick the box next to the correct answer.

   A   They were gesturing for help but couldn't be heard.   ☐

   B   They could be heard calling for help.   ☐

   C   They couldn't hear the crowd below.   ☐

   D   They were not able to speak because of the smoke.   ☐

3. Line 6 states that "Wilson's son and another man were off like a shot". Explain in your own words what this means.

   _____

4. "she had become aware of this" (lines 10-11). Which one of these words is an adjective? Tick the box next to the correct answer.

   A   this   ☐

   B   become   ☐

   C   aware   ☐

   D   she   ☐

5. Give another word or phrase that means the same as "agitated" (line 11) as it is used in the text.

   _____

6.   Find and copy a phrase from the text that means the same as 'long for'.

   _____

7.   "the rattle of the fire engine" (line 16). Which technique is used in this phrase?
     Tick the box next to the correct answer.

     A   Alliteration   ☐

     B   Personification   ☐

     C   Onomatopoeia   ☐

     D   Metaphor   ☐

8.   Why couldn't the firefighters fight the fire? Tick the box next to the correct answer.

     A   They did not arrive in time.   ☐

     B   The fire hydrants were not working.   ☐

     C   They couldn't get through the crowd.   ☐

     D   George Wilson was fighting the fire instead.   ☐

9.   Why were the girls "sick" (line 21)? Tick the box next to the correct answer.

     A   They were worried about the fire.   ☐

     B   The smoke made them feel unwell.   ☐

     C   The heat from the fire made them feel faint.   ☐

     D   They felt crushed by the crowd.   ☐

END OF TEST

/ 9

Puzzles 1

Thinking caps on! Practise your **word-type** skills with the puzzles on this page.

Concealed Conjunctions

There are six conjunctions hidden in the word search. Circle them and write them on the lines below. The first letter of each word has been given for you.

R	E	T	F	A	I	C	A
N	B	D	R	M	P	E	L
S	E	S	W	E	N	R	T
I	C	A	H	K	D	Z	H
P	A	Y	I	E	B	N	O
K	U	N	L	I	T	N	U
G	S	C	E	L	N	S	G
Z	E	K	I	D	E	T	H

w _ _ _ _

a _ _ _ _ _ _ _

a _

b _ _ _ _ _ _ _

u _ _ _ _

a _ _ _ _

Sentence Stumper

Use five of the words below to form a proper sentence that makes sense and matches the order of the word types in the blue boxes. Write your new sentence on the line.

DETERMINER	ADJECTIVE	NOUN	VERB	ADVERB

these   elegant   clockwise   the   squawked

furniture   shrilly   peacock   stayed   hollow

_____

You have **10 minutes** to do this test. Work as quickly and accurately as you can.

This passage has some punctuation mistakes.
Write the passage out again with the correct punctuation.

1.   Natalies mum kept shouting to her from the kitchen. "Get down here now,"
     Natalie plugged in her headphones and ignored her. A few moments later,
     Her mum stormed "furiously" up the stairs.

_____

_____

_____

_____

This passage contains some spelling mistakes.
Write the passage out again with the correct spellings.

2.   Parvati hadn't notised the collossal spider that was crawling over her desk. When
     she did, she screamed. She was incredibly afraid of spiders, although she knew her
     phobia was compleetly irratianal.

_____

_____

_____

_____

TURN OVER

For each numbered line, choose the word which completes the passage correctly. The passage needs to make sense and be written in correct English. Circle the correct letter.

3. Josh **wake** **waked** **woke** **woken** **waking** up to the sound of rain against his tent.
       A   B   C   D   E

4. He **touching** **feel** **touches** **touched** **feels** the roof of the tent and a pool of water
       A   B   C   D   E

5. that had collected on the top burst **at** **beneath** **through** **up** **under** onto him
       A   B   C   D   E

6. and his friends. Tim woke up, shouting **angry** **furious** **fuming** **fury** **angrily** and
       A   B   C   D   E

7. soaking wet. Somehow, Patrick was **still** **already** **soon** **later** **otherwise** asleep,
       A   B   C   D   E

8. snoring gently as the rain pounded **before** **between** **out of** **in** **against** the canvas.
       A   B   C   D   E

9. "I think we **should** **would** **need** **have** **are** get out — it's too wet and miserable in
       A   B   C   D   E

10. here," Josh said. They woke Patrick up and **leaving** **goes** **leave** **left** **gone**.
        A   B   C   D   E

END OF TEST

/ 18

Test 5: Comprehension

You have **10 minutes** to do this test. Work as quickly and accurately as you can.

Read this poem carefully and answer the questions that follow.

Wintry Tints

The sky is like an opal,
And the horizon's ring
Is yellow, like a band of gold,
To hold so rich a thing.

5   The wheat-fields are as fleecy
As any cloud that blows,
But tawny tufts of standing corn
Prick lightly through the snows.

Beside the drift-bound wind-mill
10 A pearly shadow plays
In tones of tender violet,
And vague, elusive greys.

And tinged with quiet olive
The hedges fine and bare,
15 Whose thorny masses down the road
An alien softness wear.

O, subtle chords of colour
Are fingered by the frost!
Though touched and tuned to colder key,
20 No grace of earth is lost.

For see! a deep red ruby
The opal heaven grows,
And yonder pool of ice is one
Great golden-hearted rose!

Evaleen Stein

Answer these questions about the text. You can refer back to the text if you need to.

1. "The sky is like an opal" (line 1). Which technique has been used in this phrase?

_____

TURN OVER ➡

2. Why do you think the wheat-fields are described as "fleecy" (line 5)?
   Tick the box next to the correct answer.

   A   They are covered in snow.   ☐

   B   They are flat.   ☐

   C   The narrator is looking at them from a distance.   ☐

   D   They are surrounded by mist.   ☐

3. What type of word is "standing" (line 7) as it is used in the text?

   _____

4. Which colour isn't mentioned in the text? Tick the box next to the correct answer.

   A   Grey   ☐

   B   Violet   ☐

   C   Gold   ☐

   D   Blue   ☐

5. Which of the following is not mentioned in the poem?
   Tick the box next to the correct answer.

   A   Snowdrifts beside the wind-mill   ☐

   B   Cornstalks poking through the snow   ☐

   C   Olive green hedges   ☐

   D   A rose garden by the pool   ☐

6. Which of these words is closest in meaning to "elusive" (line 12)?
   Tick the box next to the correct answer.

   A   Mysterious   ☐

   B   Confusing   ☐

   C   Dazzling   ☐

   D   Dark   ☐

7. Give another word or phrase that means the same as
   "alien" (line 16) as it is used in the text.

   _____

8. Which of the following best describes what is happening in the fifth verse?
   Tick the box next to the correct answer.

   A   Everything looks white because it's covered in frost.   ☐

   B   The poet thinks the weather is due to get even colder.   ☐

   C   Everything looks bleak and harsh in the snow.   ☐

   D   A rainbow has appeared in the wintry sky.   ☐

9. "a deep red ruby / The opal heaven grows" (lines 21-22).
   Explain what these lines mean in your own words.

   _____

   _____

END OF TEST

/ 9

Test 6: Proofreading

You have **10 minutes** to do this test. Work as quickly and accurately as you can.

> For each numbered line, choose the word which completes
> the passage correctly. The passage needs to make sense
> and be written in correct English. Circle the correct letter.

1. I **liked**   **did like**   **am liking**   **look**   **would like**   to invite you to my party on
    A   B   C   D   E

2. Friday. It's **making**   **having**   **taking**   **being**   **going**   place at my house and there
    A   B   C   D   E

3. will be a bouncy castle. Please **where**   **we're**   **wear**   **ware**   **wore**   fancy dress.
    A   B   C   D   E

4. There **will**   **ought**   **would**   **were**   **have**   be fizzy drinks, sandwiches and cake.
    A   B   C   D   E

> This passage has some punctuation mistakes.
> Write the passage out again with the correct punctuation.

5. Nigels learning to drive, but he is'nt very good. He was trying to reverse out-of his
    driveway and he knocked over his mothers plant pots He drove off quickly to avoid
    his Mum.

    _____

    _____

    _____

16

This passage contains some spelling mistakes. Each numbered line has either one mistake or no mistake. For each line, work out which group of words contains a mistake, and circle the correct letter. Circle N if there is no mistake.

6. To get to his house from school, Callum had to walk through the cemetry. Today,

     A   **B**   **C**   **D**   **N**

7. it was more frightning than ever. A cold wind swept through the graveyard, rattling

     A   **B**   **C**   **D**   **N**

8. the leaves of an ancient yew tree. Thunder could be heard in the distance and

     A   **B**   **C**   **D**   **N**

9. a flash of lightening lit up the sky. He'd forgotten his coat and was getting quite

     A   **B**   **C**   **D**   **N**

10. wet. The spooky atmosphear made him feel anxious and the hairs stood up on

     A   **B**   **C**   **D**   **N**

11. the back of his neck. Twiggs and foliage crunched under his feet and he saw a rat

     A   **B**   **C**   **D**   **N**

12. scurrying towards him. Using all of his phisical strength, he sprinted out of the

     A   **B**   **C**   **D**   **N**

13. graveyard as fast as he could and didn't stop until he had reached his front door.

     A   **B**   **C**   **D**   **N**

END OF TEST

/ 18

Test 6

These puzzles will test your knowledge of **homographs** and your **logic skills**.

Definition Link

The pairs of definitions below are linked by a single word. Fill in the gaps with a word that fits both the definition on the left and the definition on the right. One has already been done for you.

Hint: the word in the middle might have two different pronunciations.

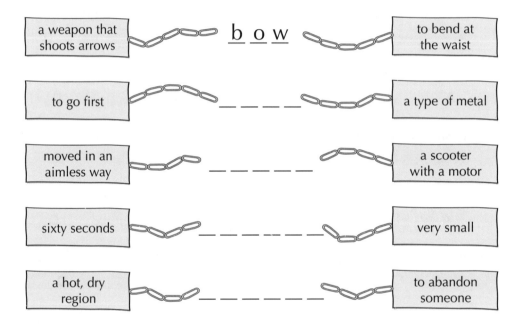

a weapon that shoots arrows	b o w	to bend at the waist
to go first	_ _ _ _	a type of metal
moved in an aimless way	_ _ _ _ _ _	a scooter with a motor
sixty seconds	_ _ _ _ _	very small
a hot, dry region	_ _ _ _ _ _	to abandon someone

Cowboy Conundrum

A cowboy rode into town on Friday.
He stayed three nights, then left on Friday.
How is this possible?

_____

_____

You have **10 minutes** to do this test. Work as quickly and accurately as you can.

Read this passage carefully and answer the questions that follow.

Sealand

Described by its rulers as 'the world's smallest nation', Sealand is a 'country' located seven miles off the coast of Suffolk.

In 1967, Major Roy Bates occupied a former naval fort in the North Sea. He wanted to set up a pirate radio station there. However, when the government made
5   it illegal for British citizens to set up off-shore pirate radio stations, he declared the site independent. It became the 'Principality of Sealand' and he crowned himself 'Prince Roy', and his wife 'Princess Joan'. He invented a flag, a national anthem and a currency: the Sealand dollar. Despite these customs being normally associated with recognised countries, established nations refuse to recognise Sealand as a
10   real country.

In 1978, crisis struck Sealand. Alexander Achenbach was a German businessman who had been granted the title of Sealand's Prime Minister for life by Prince Roy, after he'd pledged to turn Sealand into a luxury hotel and casino. But while Prince Roy and Princess Joan were away in the UK on a business trip, Achenbach flew in
15   a group of German and Dutch businessmen by helicopter to try to seize the fort. However, Prince Roy and his son, Prince Michael, retaliated. They slid down ropes from a helicopter and frightened the invaders. The invaders quickly surrendered, but Mr Achenbach's lawyer was taken hostage and a German diplomat had to be sent from the embassy in London to negotiate his release. Prince Roy perceived
20   Germany's sending of a diplomat to be an indication that Germany acknowledged Sealand as a genuine country.

1978 was the last time that Sealand faced any serious external threat. There have been several (often only half-serious) attempts to establish small countries or 'micronations'. However, these have rarely been accepted as legitimate, and few
25   have lasted as long as Sealand or have actually been embroiled in real-life conflict.

TURN OVER

> Answer these questions about the text. You can refer back to the text if you need to.

1. Why do you think the author has put quote marks around the word "country" (line 1)?

   _____

2. Why did Prince Roy originally occupy the naval fort?
   Tick the box next to the correct answer.

   A   He planned to set up his own country.   ☐

   B   He wanted to set up a radio station.   ☐

   C   As a Major, he took an interest in military things. ☐

   D   He wanted to move out of the UK.   ☐

3. "It became the 'Principality of Sealand'" (line 6).
   Which of these words is a pronoun? Tick the box next to the correct answer.

   A   It   ☐

   B   the   ☐

   C   Principality ☐

   D   of   ☐

4. Which of the following best describes Sealand?
   Tick the box next to the correct answer.

   A   A naval fort in Suffolk   ☐

   B   A luxury hotel in the North Sea   ☐

   C   An offshore radio station owned by German businessmen ☐

   D   An unrecognised offshore principality   ☐

5. Find a word from the text that means the same as 'fought back'.

_____

6. Why did Prince Roy believe that Sealand had been recognised as a country by Germany? Tick the box next to the correct answer.

    A   The German government announced their recognition.   ☐

    B   Germany sent a representative of the country to Sealand.   ☐

    C   They built an embassy on Sealand.   ☐

    D   They built a casino on Sealand.   ☐

7. "1978 was the last time that Sealand faced any serious external threat" (line 22). Explain what this means in your own words.

_____

_____

8. Give an example of how Sealand differs from most other micronations.

_____

_____

9. Give another word or phrase that means the same as "embroiled" (line 25) as it is used in the text.

_____

END OF TEST

/ 9

You have **10 minutes** to do this test. Work as quickly and accurately as you can.

> For each numbered line, choose the word which completes
> the passage correctly. The passage needs to make sense
> and be written in correct English. Circle the correct letter.

1. Terry and **me him myself I his** play in defence. It was the last game
   　　　　　A　　B　　C　　D　E

2. **by of upon on next to** the season and we couldn't afford another disastrous
   A　B　　C　　D　　E

3. defeat. The team we **were is we're was where** playing against had some of
   　　　　　　　　A　　B　　C　　D　　E

4. the **tinyest tinniest tinier tiny tiniest** players I'd ever seen.
   　　A　　　B　　　C　　　D　　E

> This passage contains some spelling mistakes.
> Write the passage out again with the correct spellings.

5. Maya hadn't expected the temprature to drop so rappidly. The mountain had
   suddenly become treacherous and she no longer felt sufficiently equiped to reach
   the summit. Difeated, she slung her bag over her sholder and trudjed back home.

_____

_____

_____

_____

This passage contains some punctuation mistakes. Each numbered line has either one mistake or no mistake. For each line, work out which group of words contains a mistake, and circle the correct letter. Circle N if there is no mistake.

6. The unrelenting weather meant that Thomas, would be stuck indoors again. It
         A   B   C   D   N

7. wasnt the first time that it had rained this week and it was becoming wearisome.
         A   B   C   D   N

8. Thomas decided to continue to work on his science project: a volcano, that
         A   B   C   D   N

9. would spew out fake lava. He couldn't wait to see the astonishment on his
         A   B   C   D   N

10. classmates faces. He imagined Mrs Robinson shrieking at the thick, orange
         A   B   C   D   N

11. sludge as it coated her desk and grinned to himself. Collecting his thoughts,
         A   B   C   D   N

12. he realised that he needed three things scissors, paper and glue. Once he'd
         A   B   C   D   N

13. assembled the volcano's structure he would then begin to cook up the lava.
         A   B   C   D   N

END OF TEST

/ 18

You have **10 minutes** to do this test. Work as quickly and accurately as you can.

Read this passage carefully and answer the questions that follow.

Jackpot

Lewis was wandering absent-mindedly through the field on his way home when he saw his 'friends' playing football. Making sure they didn't notice him, he scuttled quickly into a small wooded area adjacent to the field. He didn't want to bump into his so-called friends, whose constant teasing he could no longer write off as a
5   joke. Then, something caught his eye. A backpack, scruffy and covered in mud, lay abandoned in a patch of nettles. With so much rubbish lying around, it was a miracle that he had spotted it. He opened it slowly — he could not believe what he saw. Clumps of £20 notes bundled together with elastic bands filled the bag. It must have contained thousands of pounds. Suddenly his excitement turned to anxiety. Whose
10   money was this? Images of gangsters and thieves sprang to mind.

Against his better judgement, he grabbed the bag and carried on through the woods, when two figures burst through the bushes.

"Nice bag, Lewis," Pete scoffed. "It looks like you found it in a bin."

"Go away, Pete. I'm going home."

15   At that moment, Frank, who had been lurking behind Lewis, pushed him over and grabbed the bag, throwing it over his head to Pete like a game of piggy in the middle. Pete staggered back as he caught the bag, clearly surprised by its weight, but in his arrogance was too embarrassed to show that he would struggle to throw it back.

"Eww... This stinks," Pete said as he dropped the bag violently. Lewis quickly
20   grabbed it and clutched it against his chest like a rugby ball. Frank shoved Lewis in a muddy puddle, and they both ran off laughing.

Undeterred, Lewis hauled himself up from the puddle. By this time it was almost dark and the last thing Lewis wanted was an interrogation from his mum. He whipped the bag over his shoulder and careered home.

Answer these questions about the text. You can refer back to the text if you need to.

1. Find a word from the text that means the same as 'alongside'.

   _____

2. Explain in your own words why Lewis goes into the wooded area.

   _____

   _____

3. Which of the following is described as a "miracle" (line 6)?
   Tick the box next to the correct answer.

   A   That Lewis noticed the bag   ☐

   B   That the bag was full of money   ☐

   C   That Pete didn't open the bag   ☐

   D   That no one else had found the bag   ☐

4. Why does Lewis's excitement turn "to anxiety" (line 9)?

   _____

   _____

5. Explain why Pete doesn't throw the bag back to Frank.

   _____

   _____

TURN OVER ➡

6. "clutched it against his chest like a rugby ball" (line 20).
   What is this an example of? Tick the box next to the correct answer.

   A   Metaphor ☐

   B   Simile ☐

   C   Personification ☐

   D   Onomatopoeia ☐

7. Which of the following best describes Lewis after being pushed over?
   Tick the box next to the correct answer.

   A   Infuriated ☐

   B   Humiliated ☐

   C   Undaunted ☐

   D   Glum ☐

8. Why is Lewis keen to get home? Tick the box next to the correct answer.

   A   He is afraid Pete and Frank might come back. ☐

   B   He wants to inspect the contents of the bag in private. ☐

   C   He wants to wash the mud off of him. ☐

   D   He doesn't want to be questioned by his mother. ☐

9. Give another word or phrase that means the same as "careered" (line 24)
   as it is used in the text.

   _____

END OF TEST

/ 9

Let's pause for some puzzles that will test your **synonym** skills.

Scattered Synonyms

Complete the word chains using the words given in bold.
Each word in the chain is a synonym of the word before it.
The first one has been done for you.

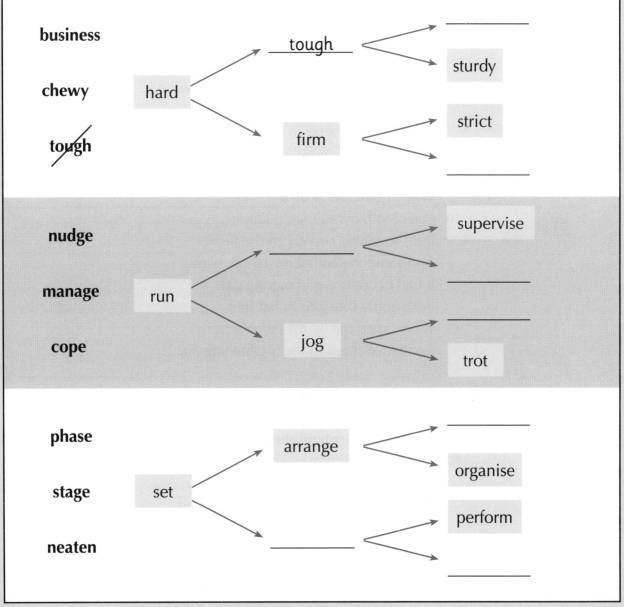

business   tough   _____

chewy   hard   sturdy

tough ~~tough~~   firm   strict

nudge   _____   supervise

manage   run   _____

cope   jog   trot

phase   arrange   _____

stage   set   organise

neaten   _____   perform

You have **10 minutes** to do this test. Work as quickly and accurately as you can.

Read this poem carefully and answer the questions that follow.

The Song of Wandering Aengus

I went out to the hazel wood,
Because a fire was in my head,
And cut and peeled a hazel wand,
And hooked a berry to a thread;
5   And when white moths were on the wing,
And moth-like stars were flickering out,
I dropped the berry in a stream
And caught a little silver trout.

When I had laid it on the floor
10 I went to blow the fire a-flame,
But something rustled on the floor,
And someone called me by my name:
It had become a glimmering girl
With apple blossom in her hair
15 Who called me by my name and ran
And faded through the brightening air.

Though I am old with wandering
Through hollow lands and hilly lands,
I will find out where she has gone,
20 And kiss her lips and take her hands;
And walk among long dappled grass,
And pluck till time and times are done,
The silver apples of the moon,
The golden apples of the sun.

W.B. Yeats

1. What person is the poem written in?

    _____

2. What does the narrator make out of the "hazel wand" (line 3) and thread?
    Tick the box next to the correct answer.

    A   A fishing rod   ☐

    B   A bow and arrow   ☐

    C   A needle and thread ☐

    D   A magic wand   ☐

3. What does the phrase "on the wing" (line 5) mean as it is used in the text?

    _____

4. What is the narrator doing when he hears his name called?

    _____

5. "glimmering girl" (line 13). What is this phrase an example of?
    Tick the box next to the correct answer.

    A   Metaphor   ☐

    B   Simile   ☐

    C   Personification ☐

    D   Alliteration   ☐

TURN OVER ➡

6. Explain in your own words where the "glimmering girl" (line 13) came from.

_____

_____

7. Why does the poet lose the girl? Tick the box next to the correct answer.

   A   She vanishes.   ☐

   B   He is too busy fishing.   ☐

   C   It is too bright and he can't see.   ☐

   D   He falls asleep.   ☐

8. "And walk among long dappled grass" (line 21).
    Which of these words is a preposition? Tick the box next to the correct answer.

   A   And   ☐

   B   dappled   ☐

   C   among   ☐

   D   grass   ☐

9. Which of the following best summarises the final verse of the poem?
    Tick the box next to the correct answer.

   A   The girl and the narrator spend the rest of their lives together.   ☐

   B   The narrator and the girl harvest fruit.   ☐

   C   The narrator and the girl walk through the grass together.   ☐

   D   The narrator still thinks about the girl even though time has passed.   ☐

END OF TEST

/ 9

Test 11: Proofreading

You have **10 minutes** to do this test. Work as quickly and accurately as you can.

> For each numbered line, choose the word which completes
> the passage correctly. The passage needs to make sense
> and be written in correct English. Circle the correct letter.

1.   Katie Jones was the person **who who's whose whom which** poem won the
                                        A   B   C   D   E

2.   poetry contest every year. I **were am would are was** suspicious because her
                                       A   B   C   D   E

3.   winning poem was never very good. I eventually figured it **up over in on out**
                                                                   A   B   C   D   E

4.   — Mr Jones, the judge, must have been **his their her our your** dad.
                                               A   B   C   D   E

> This passage contains some spelling mistakes.
> Write the passage out again with the correct spellings.

5.   Elijah was learning a foriegn langauge. He had bought a French dictionery and his
      friend had suggested that he attend an evening class to improve his pronunsation and
      comunication skills.

_____

_____

_____

_____

TURN OVER ➡

31

This passage contains some punctuation mistakes. Each numbered line has either one mistake or no mistake. For each line, work out which group of words contains a mistake, and circle the correct letter. Circle N if there is no mistake.

6. Heaving her ship off the side of the shore Karina embarked on a great adventure.
    A   **B**   **C**   **D**   **N**

7. Shed packed all the essentials: lemons, papaya and oranges (to prevent her from
    A   **B**   **C**   **D**   **N**

8. getting scurvy. Karina had heard many tales about pirates, so she remembered
    A   **B**   **C**   **D**   **N**

9. to pack her sword, which had been fashioned from a long and pointy tree branch
    A   **B**   **C**   **D**   **N**

10. "Aha," she exclaimed, jumping onto shore. "I've spotted an enemy. En garde"!
    A   **B**   **C**   **D**   **N**

11. She held her sword to her dog's chin, who barked and then strolled off grumpily.
    A   **B**   **C**   **D**   **N**

12. Karinas' older brother, Anton, gave an exasperated sigh and rolled his eyes as he
    A   **B**   **C**   **D**   **N**

13. watched his sister sail, around the duck pond in a dinghy, lost in her own world.
    A   **B**   **C**   **D**   **N**

END OF TEST

/ 18

Test 12: Comprehension

You have **10 minutes** to do this test. Work as quickly and accurately as you can.

Read this passage carefully and answer the questions that follow.

The Traveller

The traveller let out a despondent sigh, keen for a place to rest his head. He had been walking for days without proper shelter and only had a few pitiful rations in his bag for sustenance. He sat astride a moss-covered stone, pulled off his boot and tipped out the pool of water that had accumulated at the bottom of it. His feet were
5   completely sodden and covered in a crop of angry blisters.

As he gazed out at the stretch of land before him, the sun began its descent and painted the sky with a lively palette of red and purple hues. The traveller shuddered at the thought of having to spend another night curled up by the fire with only the distant howls of wolves for company. As the sun dipped lower, the temperature
10   plummeted, and the traveller knew that he would have to find shelter swiftly.

But as darkness began to fall, he was yet to find a suitable place to rest. The desolate moorland was completely exposed to the elements, and the boggy terrain, although not uncomfortable, was saturated with water. The traveller didn't know which animals called this place home, but he hoped they were friendly.
15   He decided to admit defeat — it would be folly to continue walking on this treacherous moor. One misplaced step might result in a twisted ankle, or worse. As he laid his head on a grassy knoll and stared up at the inky blackness, his thoughts turned to the reason for his journey. His brother was returning from a war overseas, and the traveller wanted to be at the port to welcome him as the boat
20   docked. The traveller's heart swelled at the thought; it had been almost three years since he had seen his brother. Would they still recognise one another? Would he still have a jovial demeanour, or would the brutality of war have changed him?

TURN OVER

Answer these questions about the text. You can refer back to the text if you need to.

1. Line 1 states that the traveller "let out a despondent sigh". What does this suggest about the traveller? Tick the box next to the correct answer.

   A   He was relieved.   ☐

   B   He was weary.   ☐

   C   He was out of breath.   ☐

   D   He was disheartened.   ☐

2. Give another word or phrase that means the same as "accumulated" (line 4) as it is used in the text.

   _____

3. Find and copy an example of personification from the text.

   _____

   _____

4. Which of the following is not given as a reason why the moor is an unsuitable place to rest? Tick the box next to the correct answer.

   A   The ground is wet.   ☐

   B   It offers no protection from bad weather.   ☐

   C   The ground is uncomfortable.   ☐

   D   There may be dangerous wild animals.   ☐

5. Explain in your own words why the traveller decides to stop walking in line 15.

   _____

   _____

6. "As he laid his head on a grassy knoll" (line 17). Which of these words is a
   determiner? Tick the box next to the correct answer.

   A   As   ☐

   B   he   ☐

   C   on   ☐

   D   a   ☐

7. Explain what the phrase "The traveller's heart swelled" (line 20) means.

   _____

   _____

8. "Would they still recognise each other?" (line 21).
   What is this an example of? Tick the box next to the correct answer.

   A   A simile   ☐

   B   A rhetorical question   ☐

   C   An idiom   ☐

   D   A metaphor   ☐

9. Find a word from the text that means the same as 'cordial'.

   _____

END OF TEST

/ 9

Thinking caps on! This page will put your **vocabulary** and **word-making** skills to the test.

Say What You See

Use the visual clues below to create six compound words.

One part of the word is given to you, but you need to work out the second part by looking at how the word is presented.

EXAMPLE:

NOTEBOOK

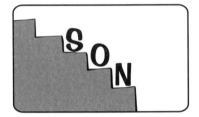

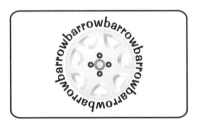

_____

_____

BONE

_____

_____

You have **10 minutes** to do this test. Work as quickly and accurately as you can.

For each numbered line, choose the word which completes the passage correctly. The passage needs to make sense and be written in correct English. Circle the correct letter.

1. "**Whose Who's Who Which Whom** diary is this?" Mr Jackson asked. Harriet
    A   B   C   D   E

2. gulped. She **didn't won't hadn't hasn't weren't** intended for anyone else to
    A   B   C   D   E

3. read it. She had **writed wrote writen write written** some mean things about
    A   B   C   D   E

4. Mr Jackson. She nervously **took had put did went** her hand up.
    A   B   C   D   E

This passage contains some spelling mistakes.
Write the passage out again with the correct spellings.

5. Rover the dog was a rascle. Wagging his tale and looking proud of himself, Mrs Bradshaw knew he'd been up to no good. She imediately entered the dinning room and screamed. Her priceless vase had been shatterred. Rover was a nusance.

_____

_____

_____

_____

TURN OVER ➡

This passage contains some punctuation mistakes. Each numbered line has either one mistake or no mistake. For each line, work out which group of words contains a mistake, and circle the correct letter. Circle N if there is no mistake.

6. Huffing and puffing in annoyance Devendra fell back in his chair. He gazed

    A   B   C   D   N

7. longingly out of the window. His house overlooked the park where his friends

    A   B   C   D   N

8. were playing football. His two best friends Kieran and Andrew, caught his eye.

    A   B   C   D   N

9. "Are you coming? they called. He explained why he wasn't able to come out.

    A   B   C   D   N

10. "I've been grounded for coming home late," he said, pretending to laugh. I'll

    A   B   C   D   N

11. be allowed out again in a week" It was torturous having to watch his friends

    A   B   C   D   N

12. have fun while he was stuck inside. He slammed the window shut and drew

    A   B   C   D   N

13. the curtains. He slumped back in his chair, sulking and watching the clock

    A   B   C   D   N

END OF TEST

/ 18

You have **10 minutes** to do this test. Work as quickly and accurately as you can.

Read this passage carefully and answer the questions that follow.

The English Samurai

Born in England in 1564, William Adams was a navigator* who initially forged a career with the Royal Navy. Since England was at war with Spain and Portugal, Adams was no stranger to naval battles and he was part of the fleet which fought the Spanish Armada in 1588.

5   In June 1598, Adams was hired by a Dutch company to travel to Japan and establish a Dutch trade post* there. The journey was gruelling, and out of the five ships that set off from Rotterdam, only Adams's reached its destination. They landed on the southern Japanese island of Kyushu in April 1600.

    When the crew arrived ashore, Portuguese missionaries* who were living in Japan
10 said that the crew were pirates and should be executed immediately. Instead, the soon-to-be leader of Japan, Tokugawa Ieyasu, ordered that they should be imprisoned.

    When Ieyasu met with the prisoners, he was impressed with Adams's shipbuilding and navigation skills, and he refused the demands for his execution. Adams wanted to return to England, where he had a wife and children, but Ieyasu refused to let him
15 leave Japan. Ieyasu promoted Adams to the class of samurai — an upper-class warrior. He gave him the name "Miura Anjin", which allowed him to remarry, as well as a large estate with 80-90 servants and a large salary.

    Anjin never went back to England and he married a Japanese woman who bore him two children. He helped to build the first western-style ships in Japan, as well as
20 allowing the Dutch and English to set up trading posts for the first time.

    However, Ieyasu's successor, Tokugawa Hidetada, began limiting Japan's trade with the outside world. Eventually, after Adams's death, only one Dutch trade post was allowed and all other foreigners in Japan were sentenced to death.

* navigator — *person who directs a ship*
* trade post — *a settlement where goods are traded*
* missionary — *someone who has been sent abroad to teach their religion*

TURN OVER

                 Test 14

Answer these questions about the text. You can refer back to the text if you need to.

1. "Adams was hired by a Dutch company" (line 5). Which of these words is a preposition? Tick the box next to the correct answer.

    A   was   ☐

    B   hired   ☐

    C   by   ☐

    D   a   ☐

2. Give another word or phrase that means the same as "gruelling" (line 6) as it is used in the text.

   _____

3. Approximately how long did it take Adams to get from Rotterdam to Japan? Tick the box next to the correct answer.

    A   Almost two years   ☐

    B   Over two years   ☐

    C   Almost ten years   ☐

    D   Almost 36 years   ☐

4. Why did the Portuguese missionaries want Adams and his crew to be executed?

   _____

   _____

5. Explain in your own words why Ieyasu refused to execute Adams.

   _____

   _____

6.	Why was Adams allowed to remarry? Tick the box next to the correct answer.

	A	His wife in England died.	☐

	B	He lost touch with his English wife.	☐

	C	In Japan, men can have two wives.	☐

	D	He changed his name.	☐

7.	Which of these things did Adams not do in Japan?
	Tick the box next to the correct answer.

	A	Help set up trading posts	☐

	B	Help Japan build ships	☐

	C	Have children	☐

	D	Fight against the Spanish Armada	☐

8.	Which of the following statements is true? Tick the box next to the correct answer.

	A	Tokugawa Ieyasu agreed to let Adams return to England.	☐

	B	The English and Dutch were at war at the time of Adams's voyage.	☐

	C	Ultimately, only the Dutch were allowed to trade in Japan.	☐

	D	Ieyasu succeeded Hidetada as leader of Japan.	☐

9.	Find a word from the text that means the same as 'restricting'.

	_____

END OF TEST

/ 9

You have **10 minutes** to do this test. Work as quickly and accurately as you can.

This passage contains some spelling mistakes.
Write the passage out again with the correct spellings.

1.   Rachid dispised eating vegetebles. His mother said it was rediculous that he wouldn't even try them. It didn't matter if brocoli, spinach, sweetcorn or peas were put in front of him — he couldn't stomac any of them.

_____

_____

_____

_____

This passage has some punctuation mistakes.
Write the passage out again with the correct punctuation.

2.   Come on, Jess shouted the crowd as Jess got nearer to the finish line. She hadnt expected to do so well, in the cross-country race.

_____

_____

_____

For each numbered line, choose the word which completes the passage correctly. The passage needs to make sense and be written in correct English. Circle the correct letter.

3. Jodie and Charlotte lived **near   next   across   around   by**   door to each other
                                      A   B   C   D   E

4. and **were   had   would   might   can**   always been best friends. They were both
           A   B   C   D   E

5. devastated that Charlotte was moving house. **Them   Then   They're   They   Their**
                                                    A   B   C   D   E

6. vowed to spend their last week together **done   does   did   doing   do**   what they
                                                A   B   C   D   E

7. enjoyed the most — **sunbathing   sunbathe   sunbatheing   sunbathed   sunbathes**.
                            A   B   C   D   E

8. When the day of the move **come   comes   go   came   went**,   they couldn't stop
                                 A   B   C   D   E

9. **cries   cry   cried   cryed   crying**. Jodie's mum looked confused.
       A   B   C   D   E

10. "Why the fuss? We **will   were   are   have   be**   only moving around the corner."
                         A   B   C   D   E

END OF TEST

/ 18

Time for a break! These puzzles will test your **word-meaning** and **synonym** skills.

Confusing Crossword

Complete the crossword using the clues below. Make sure you get the correct word type that the clue is asking for.

Across

3. A verb related to 'suggestion'.

5. A verb related to 'escape'.

6. An adverb related to 'precise'.

Down

1. A noun related to 'experience'.

2. A noun related to 'help'.

4. An adjective related to 'cautiously'.

Merry Mix-Up

Unscramble the following words and write the correct spelling on the line below.

Hint: three of the words are a synonym of the word 'happy'.

U E L G F E L

O J U L F Y

F R E E U L C H

X I T C E D E

One word has a slightly different meaning to the others.

Which is the odd word out? _____

You have **10 minutes** to do this test. Work as quickly and accurately as you can.

Read this passage carefully and answer the questions that follow.

An adapted extract from 'In Search of the Okapi'

He was asleep, and he was awake again so suddenly that he did not know he had slept until he saw that his rifle had moved. The jackal plucked at his blanket. He remembered that something had disturbed him, and he judged that the jackal had done the same thing just before. He yawned and patted its head; but, instead of sitting
5 down, it ran a few yards, sniffed the air, whined, came back, glanced long over its shoulder into the riverbed, looked into Venning's face, then ran off in the direction of the camp. As soon as it was gone Venning felt lonely.

He stood up, thinking to return to the camp, then sat down again, for he heard the sharp stamp that an antelope makes when alarmed, and he hoped to see it come into
10 the moonlight. So he settled down to watch again, and drowsiness fell upon his eyes. He could see the white patch of sand, and as his heavy lids were lowered and lifted between the drowsy intervals, he became dimly conscious that there was something on the sand. Yes; there it was, something grey, short, and thick. A donkey, he told himself. He smiled sleepily. A donkey!

15 It was strange to see the old familiar form out there in the wilderness. He wondered dreamily where it came from; then a shadow cast by the moon on a passing cloud blotted out the river-bed. He rubbed his eyes, and when the cloud had gone there were two animals — donkeys, unmistakably — one larger than the other, both with their heads turned upwards towards him. Another cloud sailed by, and when it had
20 passed he missed them, and, his curiosity roused, he rubbed his eyes again for a closer scrutiny. Surely that was not a bush on the bank? No! it moved. The donkeys were coming towards him. One of them, the larger, moved forward quickly, then stopped. Then a chill ran through him, his heart grew weak, his breathing grew sharp, and the sweat suddenly started out all over his face and body. That was no donkey standing
25 there, with its huge head now sunk almost to the ground, now lifted high, as it tried to make out what manner of living creature it was crouching there by the rock above!

Ernest Glanville

TURN OVER ➡

45   Test 16

1. What makes Venning realise he had fallen asleep?
    Tick the box next to the correct answer.

    A   The position of the blanket has changed. ☐

    B   He didn't notice the jackal arrive. ☐

    C   The position of his gun has changed. ☐

    D   He has a dream about donkeys. ☐

2. In your own words, explain how the reader can tell something is wrong from the
    jackal's behaviour in lines 4-7.

    _____

    _____

3. In line 8, Venning thinks about returning to the camp. Why does he decide to stay
    where he is instead?

    _____

4. Which of the following words best describes Venning's reaction when he thinks
    the figure on the sand is a donkey? Tick the box next to the correct answer.

    A   Alarmed ☐

    B   Relieved ☐

    C   Amused ☐

    D   Distraught ☐

5. Line 17 states that the river-bed was "blotted out" by a passing cloud.
    Explain in your own words what this means.

    _____

    _____

6. Find a word from the text that means the same as 'inspection'.

    _____

7. Which of the following statements is false?
    Tick the box next to the correct answer.

    A   It is night-time when Venning spots the creatures.   ☐

    B   The creatures are both the same size.   ☐

    C   Venning is positioned above the creatures.   ☐

    D   The creatures approach Venning.   ☐

8. "a chill ran through him" (line 23).
    Which word in this phrase is a pronoun?

    _____

9. "huge head" (line 25). What is this phrase an example of?
    Tick the box next to the correct answer.

    A   Metaphor   ☐

    B   Simile   ☐

    C   Personification   ☐

    D   Alliteration   ☐

END OF TEST

/ 9

You have **10 minutes** to do this test. Work as quickly and accurately as you can.

For each numbered line, choose the word which completes the passage correctly. The passage needs to make sense and be written in correct English. Circle the correct letter.

1. Kirsty was incredibly nervous to **say   spoke   saying   speak   speaking** in front of
     A B C D E

2. the **most   majority   whole   all   part** school. She was not very confident or
     A B C D E

3. outgoing, so **get   stood   climbing   getting   standing** at the front in assembly was
     A B C D E

4. one of her **worst   worse   best   least   good** nightmares.
     A B C D E

This passage contains some spelling mistakes.
Write the passage out again with the correct spellings.

5. Joel was perched on a bench eating his sausage roll when he heard a perculiar noise. Seagles were screaching overhead and started to harrass him for his food. They were especialy aggressive and gave him no oportunity to escape.

_____

_____

_____

_____

48

This passage contains some punctuation mistakes. Each numbered line has either one mistake or no mistake. For each line, work out which group of words contains a mistake, and circle the correct letter. Circle N if there is no mistake.

6. often nicknamed 'sea parrots' because they have colourful beaks, puffins are

   A B C D N

7. unique seabirds. You can find puffins on a few small islands around Britain:

   A B C D N

8. Fair Isle, Shetland and Orkney, Scotland; the Farne Islands England; and South

   A B C D N

9. Stack, Wales, They are excellent divers and can dive up to 60m underwater to

   A B C D N

10. find their favourite food — fish. When they are breeding, the female will lay

    A B C D N

11. one egg in a burrow and both parents' look after the egg until it hatches. Puffins

    A B C D N

12. spend eight months of the year fishing at sea. During this time their distinctive

    A B C D N

13. colourful beaks turn grey. Its difficult to recognise them without their colour.

    A B C D N

END OF TEST

/ 18

You have **10 minutes** to do this test. Work as quickly and accurately as you can.

Read this poem carefully and answer the questions that follow.

The Redbreast

Cold blew the freezing northern blast,
And winter sternly frowned;
The flaky snow fell thick and fast,
And clad the fields around.

5   Forced by the storm's relentless power,
Emboldened by despair,
A shivering redbreast* sought my door,
Some friendly warmth to share.

'Welcome, sweet bird!' I fondly cried,
10 'No danger need you fear,
Secure with me you may abide,
Till warmer suns appear.

'And when mild spring comes smiling on,
And bids the fields look gay*,
15 You, with your sweet, your grateful song,
My kindness shall repay.'

Mistaken thought! — But how shall I
The mournful truth display?
An envious cat, with jealous eye,
20   Had marked him as her prey.

Remorseless wretch! — her cruel jaws
Soon sealed her victim's doom,
While I in silence mourn his loss,
And weep over robin's tomb.

25   So, oft in life's uneven way,
Some stroke may intervene;
Sweep all our fancied joys away,
And change the flattering scene.

Charlotte Richardson

* redbreast — *robin*
* gay — *cheerful*

1. Find a phrase from the first verse which contains personification.

    _____

    _____

2. Lines 3-4 state, "The flaky snow fell thick and fast, / And clad the fields around."
    Explain in your own words what this means.

    _____

    _____

3. Give another word or phrase that means the same as "relentless" (line 5).

    _____

4. Why does the robin come to the narrator's door?
    Tick the box next to the correct answer.

    A   The storm blew away its nest.   ☐

    B   It wants to come in from the cold.   ☐

    C   There is food in the house.   ☐

    D   The narrator is trying to attract robins to their house.   ☐

5. The narrator wants the bird to stay with them until...
    Tick the box next to the correct answer.

    A   the morning.   ☐

    B   the weather gets warmer.   ☐

    C   the cat arrives.   ☐

    D   the summer.   ☐

TURN OVER ➡

6. How does the narrator expect the robin to pay them back?

_____

_____

7. Give another word or phrase that means the same as "mournful" (line 18).

_____

8. According to the poet, why does the cat kill the robin?
   Tick the box next to the correct answer.

   A   She wants to eat the bird.   ☐

   B   She begrudges the bird.   ☐

   C   She is angry at the bird.   ☐

   D   She is upset with the bird.   ☐

9. What lesson does the narrator take from the robin's death?
   Tick the box next to the correct answer.

   A   Your life can change unexpectedly at any time.   ☐

   B   Always be kind to strangers.   ☐

   C   Protect wildlife and the environment.   ☐

   D   Never let strangers into your home.   ☐

END OF TEST

/ 9

Time for a break! These puzzles are a great way to practise your **word-making** skills.

Match the Mice

Draw a line to connect each of the mice with the piece of cheese that will turn their verb into a noun. For the mice that are already connected to a piece of cheese, write a new verb that would be a correct match.

One of the mice doesn't match with a piece of cheese.
What noun can you turn this verb into? _____

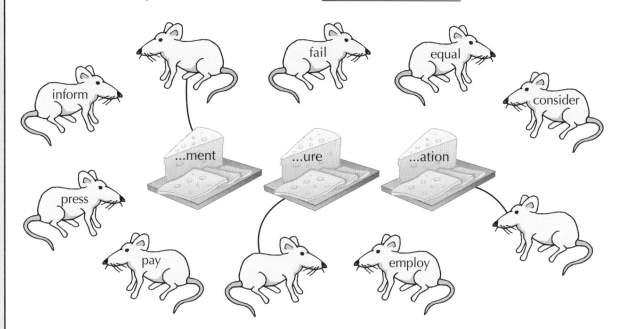

Antonym Anagrams

Unscramble the anagrams below — each one is an antonym of the word beneath it in brackets. Write the unscrambled word on the line below.

A R P I L Y D   M I L P E S   T O U R F T E A N

(slowly)   (complicated)   (unlucky)

_ _ _ _ _ _ _   _ _ _ _ _ _   _ _ _ _ _ _ _ _ _

You have **10 minutes** to do this test. Work as quickly and accurately as you can.

For each numbered line, choose the word, or group of words, which completes the passage correctly. The passage needs to make sense and be written in correct English. Circle the correct letter.

1. The dog was dashing around the garden, chasing **there its it's they're it** tail.
    A   B   C   D   E

2. Suddenly, it **fell falls fallen fall fells** over. Panting, it ran up to its owner,
    A   B   C   D   E

3. Natalie. Natalie **shake shook shaken shakes shaked** her head disapprovingly.
    A   B   C   D   E

4. She thought she had the **stupid crazy crazier craziest stupider** dog ever.
    A   B   C   D   E

This passage has some punctuation mistakes.
Write the passage out again with the correct punctuation.

5. Simon wore large sun-glasses, and a hood so that nobody would recognise him.
    "Simon! Simon! Someone, shouted", blowing his cover.

    _____

    _____

    _____

This passage contains some spelling mistakes. Each numbered line has either one mistake or no mistake. For each line, work out which group of words contains a mistake, and circle the correct letter. Circle N if there is no mistake.

6. Pablo sat in his mum's car as the rain hammerred against the window constantly.

         A   **B**   **C**   **D**   **N**

7. Vehicals were crawling at an unusually slow pace — Pablo hoped he wouldn't be

         A   **B**   **C**   **D**   **N**

8. late for school. Soon, they came to a complete stop. Up ahead, a sign read: "Due

         A   **B**   **C**   **D**   **N**

9. to adverse weather condissions, the bridge has been closed." Pablo let out a loud

         A   **B**   **C**   **D**   **N**

10. grown. There was another bridge that he could cross further into the village, but

         A   **B**   **C**   **D**   **N**

11. because of the trafic, the car wasn't going anywhere any time soon. Reluctantly,

         A   **B**   **C**   **D**   **N**

12. Pablo grabbed his bag, hugged his mum and stepped out into the pooring rain.

         A   **B**   **C**   **D**   **N**

13. He eventually turned up to school over an hour late and completely drenched.

         A   **B**   **C**   **D**   **N**

END OF TEST

/ 18

You have **10 minutes** to do this test. Work as quickly and accurately as you can.

Read this passage carefully and answer the questions that follow.

Holmwood Manor

Heavy oak doors flanked by stained glass panels greeted Elizabeth on her arrival at Holmwood Manor. She hammered on the door with gusto, but only managed to produce a muted tap. Being unused to such large houses and mindful of her manners, she stepped off the huge stone step and waited patiently for a response.

5   At that moment, the door, as if by magic, swung wide open and an elderly man appeared. Elizabeth thought that she had never seen someone who looked so old. His complete lack of hair revealed a huge, oddly-shaped head. Elizabeth wondered how a body so thin and brittle could ever prop up such a large head. His skin had an unhealthy, yellowish tinge; he looked so sickly that Elizabeth was unsure how he

10   managed to remain standing. Remembering her manners, however, she stretched her hand out to greet him.

"Hello, you must be Mr Holmwood. I saw your cleaning vacancy advertised in the gazette." Elizabeth rambled and mumbled her words, concerned about whether the man was scrutinising her shabby cloak.

15   "You are mistaken," he replied solemnly, barely moving his thin lips. "I am Mr Jenkins, the butler. Mr Holmwood will not be joining us this evening."

Elizabeth could sense no hint of emotion, positive or negative, in his voice. She followed him through the long and winding corridors of the manor, during which he didn't utter a word. As she followed the shuffling Mr Jenkins, Elizabeth's mouth was

20   agape, her eyes flickering around in childlike awe at her surroundings. Eventually he brought her to a large dining room — she had never seen a room look so grand and yet so dilapidated. Everything was covered in a thick layer of dust, which added to Elizabeth's burgeoning sense of unease.

Answer the following questions about the text. You can refer back to the text if you need to.

1. Find a word from the text that means the same as 'conscious'.

   _____

2. Why does Elizabeth step off the "huge stone step" (line 4)?
   Tick the box next to the correct answer.

   A   The house makes her feel anxious.   ☐

   B   She wants to get out of the way of the opening doors.   ☐

   C   She is being polite.   ☐

   D   She wants to peer through the stained glass panels.   ☐

3. "I saw your cleaning vacancy advertised in the gazette" (lines 12-13).
   Which of these words is a determiner? Tick the box next to the correct answer.

   A   I   ☐

   B   cleaning   ☐

   C   in   ☐

   D   the   ☐

4. Explain in your own words why Elizabeth mumbles when she speaks to Mr Jenkins.

   _____

   _____

5. Give another word or phrase that means the same as "solemnly" (line 15).

   _____

TURN OVER ➡

6. Which word could not be used to describe Mr Jenkins?
   Tick the box next to the correct answer.

   A   Fragile   ☐

   B   Quiet   ☐

   C   Serious   ☐

   D   Angry   ☐

7. How does Elizabeth feel as she is walking through the corridors?
   Tick the box next to the correct answer.

   A   Amazed   ☐

   B   Delighted   ☐

   C   Horrified   ☐

   D   Excited   ☐

8. "she had never seen a room look so grand and yet so dilapidated" (lines 21-22).
   What does this mean? Tick the box next to the correct answer.

   A   She had never seen a dirtier room.   ☐

   B   The room was full of beautiful things which were elegantly arranged.   ☐

   C   The room was full of impressive things, but looked neglected.   ☐

   D   The room was shabby but welcoming.   ☐

9. "added to Elizabeth's burgeoning sense of unease" (lines 22-23).
   Explain what this means in your own words.

   _____

   _____

END OF TEST

/ 9

Test 21: Proofreading

You have **10 minutes** to do this test. Work as quickly and accurately as you can.

This passage contains some spelling mistakes.
Write the passage out again with the correct spellings.

1. Fiona was an exellent actor and she was audisioning for the lead roll in the school
    play. She was doutful that she would get it, though: Caley always got the best
    caracters.

    _____

    _____

    _____

    _____

This passage has some punctuation mistakes.
Write the passage out again with the correct punctuation.

2. "Shh! the librarian" said, far more loudly than anyone, was actually speaking.
    Olivia was only asking Matty whether hed read a certain book: 'Hopscotch and
    Bedrock' by simon Winner.

    _____

    _____

    _____

TURN OVER

3. Cian wanted to impress **their his mine the that** mum and thought it would
    　　　　　　　　　　　　　　A　　B　　C　　D　　E

4. **be is are were being** a nice idea to make dinner for the family. However,
    A　B　C　　D　　　E

5. he didn't know **which why how who whose** to cook and he wasn't
    　　　　　　　　　　A　　B　　C　　D　　E

6. **permit permitting allowed allows couldn't** to use the hob. He opened the
    　　A　　　B　　　　C　　　D　　　E

7. fridge, and it was largely empty **accept other apart despite instead** from
    　　　　　　　　　　　　　　　　A　　B　　C　　D　　E

8. half a mouldy onion, **some a one that any** mustard and a stalk of celery.
    　　　　　　　　　　　A　B　C　D　E

9. Since he had so **much little enough few less** food to work with, he
    　　　　　　　　　A　　B　　C　　D　E

10. **decided decides deciding decide decider** to order a takeaway instead.
    　A　　　B　　　C　　　D　　　E

END OF TEST

/ 18

Have a go at these puzzles which test your knowledge of **spelling** and **punctuation**.

Cube Clues

Work out the answers to the clues below using only the letters in the cube. Each letter can only be used once in each word and each word must contain the letter 'R'.

U	F	S
N	R	O
W	L	E

someone who works in a hospital _____

a word meaning 'further down' _____

a word meaning 'scowl' _____

an adjective meaning 'certain' _____

Can you unscramble the nine-letter word?   _ _ _ _ _ _ _ _ _

Hint: it's a type of plant.

Crack the Code

Today is June's first day as a secret agent, and her first challenge is getting into the office. The code for the front door is hidden in the message below.

Its horrable weather we're having, isn't it? It rained all of yesterday and I got drenched on my way home from work I hope it will have improved by tomorrow — Im sick of everything looking so miserible.

June has been given the first number of the code but needs to find the final two. Count the spelling mistakes and punctuation mistakes in the message and write the code in the space below.

The door code is: _6_ ___ ___

spelling mistakes   punctuation mistakes

You have **10 minutes** to do this test. Work as quickly and accurately as you can.

For each numbered line, choose the word, or group of words,
which completes the passage correctly. The passage needs to make
sense and be written in correct English. Circle the correct letter.

1. Mrs Hughes was **get gotten got gets getting** ready to finally put her feet up.
    A   B   C   D   E

2. She'd spent all week looking **at after with over around** four small children
    A   B   C   D   E

3. single-handedly. She made **your their herself his her** a cup of tea when
    A   B   C   D   E

4. **although during because of due to suddenly** all four children started crying!
    A   B   C   D   E

This passage contains some spelling mistakes.
Write the passage out again with the correct spellings.

5. Daniel freqently walked passed the bike shop in town. He was desparate for a new
    bike, but he couldn't afford one. One day, there was a bike in the shop window
    which was redused by fourty pounds. What a bargin!

    _____

    _____

    _____

    _____

This passage contains some punctuation mistakes. Each numbered line has either one mistake or no mistake. For each line, work out which group of words contains a mistake, and circle the correct letter. Circle N if there is no mistake.

6. Callum and Louise never stopped arguing, Vicky couldn't believe she was
          A   **B**   **C**   **D**   **N**

7. going on holiday with them. They were on their way, to the airport and they'd
        A   **B**   **C**   **D**   **N**

8. already started bickering, between themselves. They were sharing a suitcase
        A   **B**   **C**   **D**   **N**

9. and this — much to Vicky's surprise — was the source of all their argument's.
        A   **B**   **C**   **D**   **N**

10. "Youve packed so much! I couldn't fit my beach towels in!" Louise snapped.
        A   **B**   **C**   **D**   **N**

11. "Why did you need to take so many clothes! We're only going for a week!"
        A   **B**   **C**   **D**   **N**

12. Louise tutted: scoffed and turned away, making sure to give Callum an angry glare.
        A   **B**   **C**   **D**   **N**

13. Vicky kept silent the whole way she didn't want to cause any more arguments.
        A   **B**   **C**   **D**   **N**

END OF TEST

/ 18

You have **10 minutes** to do this test. Work as quickly and accurately as you can.

> Read this passage carefully and answer the questions that follow.

Languages of the United Kingdom

Some people think that the UK is an entirely English-speaking nation. Although it's true that English is spoken by the vast majority of the population on a day-to-day basis, there are lots of other languages that are used throughout the UK.

One notable language is Welsh, which is used mostly in the north and west of
5   Wales. It has around 700 000 speakers, including about 20% of the population of Wales. Welsh is a Celtic language which is completely unlike English. Although a similar language to Welsh was once spoken across much of England, it died out when England was invaded by Anglo-Saxons hundreds of years ago and the English people adopted the language of the invaders. Welsh is a thriving language with a bright
10 future — in 2010, the Welsh Assembly passed measures to develop and protect it.

In a few areas, such as the Outer Hebrides of Scotland, another Celtic language, Scottish Gaelic, is spoken. It is closely related to Irish, which is spoken by some people in Northern Ireland, and it has around 57 000 speakers. Today, many children in these areas are educated entirely in Gaelic in an attempt to breathe life into the
15 language.

A lesser-known Celtic language also spoken in the UK is Cornish — it has far fewer speakers than either Welsh or Gaelic. Cornwall retained a distinct identity from the rest of England into the Middle Ages, but by the 19th century, many believe that Cornish had died out completely. Recently, efforts have been made to revive the
20 Cornish language — enthusiasts have learnt Cornish from old sources, and written dictionaries and grammars in the hope of preserving it. There are still very few people who are brought up speaking Cornish, but a Cornish language crèche opened in 2010.

Of course, these are not the only languages you can hear on the streets of the UK. People from all over the world have brought their languages to the UK's shores. The
25 most common immigrant language is Polish, with around 500 000 speakers.

Answer these questions about the text. You can refer back to the text if you need to.

1. According to the text, which of these statements about the Welsh language is true? Tick the box next to the correct answer.

   A   Welsh is used less in the south and east of Wales.   ☐

   B   More people in Wales speak Welsh than English.   ☐

   C   The Welsh language is related to English.   ☐

   D   Welsh has fewer speakers than Scottish Gaelic.   ☐

2. "a similar language to Welsh was once spoken across much of England" (lines 6-7). Explain in your own words why this is not the case any more.

   _____

   _____

3. Why do you think the Welsh language has a "bright future" (lines 9-10)?

   _____

4. What does the phrase "to breathe life into" (line 14) mean?

   _____

5. What do you think the phrase "retained a distinct identity" (line 17) means?

   _____

   _____

TURN OVER ➡

6. Which of the following statements is false?
   Tick the box next to the correct answer.

   A Cornish is a Celtic language. ☐

   B More people in Britain speak Polish than Cornish. ☐

   C People think that Cornish died out in the 1900s. ☐

   D Cornish was more widely spoken in the Middle Ages. ☐

7. "Recently, efforts have been made to revive the Cornish language" (lines 19-20).
   Which of these words is an adverb?

   _____

8. Why do you think a Cornish language crèche was opened?
   Tick the box next to the correct answer.

   A To increase the number of Cornish-speaking children. ☐

   B To prevent Cornish children from learning English. ☐

   C To encourage more people to buy Cornish dictionaries. ☐

   D Because Cornish children were struggling to understand English. ☐

9. "People from all over the world have brought their languages to the UK's shores"
   (line 24). What does this sentence mean? Tick the box next to the correct answer.

   A Foreign languages are more commonly found near the UK's coast. ☐

   B There are more languages spoken in the UK than anywhere else. ☐

   C People in the UK are taught to speak at least two languages. ☐

   D Lots of different languages are spoken in the UK. ☐

END OF TEST

/ 9

You have **10 minutes** to do this test. Work as quickly and accurately as you can.

For each numbered line, choose the word, or group of words,
which completes the passage correctly. The passage needs to make
sense and be written in correct English. Circle the correct letter.

1. **I was   I   I will   I would   I have** planning to take the dog for a walk in the hills
    [A]   [B]   [C]   [D]   [E]

2. this weekend, but the weather is so awful I **do   doesn't   will   don't   won't** think
                                                 [A]   [B]   [C]   [D]   [E]

3. I want to. We'll just have to go for a walk **over   next   around   among   out** the
                                                  [A]   [B]   [C]   [D]   [E]

4. corner instead and save the hills for **following   after   next   before   last** weekend.
                                           [A]   [B]   [C]   [D]   [E]

This passage has some punctuation mistakes.
Write the passage out again with the correct punctuation.

5. Were going to Manchester my home town) this weekend, I'm looking forward to
    seeing my family, but I'm sure, well end up arguing — we always do?

    _____

    _____

    _____

TURN OVER ➡

This passage contains some spelling mistakes. Each numbered line has either one mistake or no mistake. For each line, work out which group of words contains a mistake, and circle the correct letter. Circle N if there is no mistake.

6. Yesterday, a profesional musician visited our school to teach us about different

   A   **B**   **C**   **D**   **N**

7. musical instruments. She told us that it had always been her dream to play for a

   A   **B**   **C**   **D**   **N**

8. world-famous orchestra. When she was younger, she had to make many sacrifises

   A   **B**   **C**   **D**   **N**

9. to achieve her ambition. She said that it was necessery for any aspiring musicians

   A   **B**   **C**   **D**   **N**

10. to have a good sense of ryhthm, plenty of discipline and a passion for music.

   A   **B**   **C**   **D**   **N**

11. Our class was allowed to try some different instruments, but it was disasterous!

   A   **B**   **C**   **D**   **N**

12. I tried to play the cello, but I didn't support it properley and it toppled over on to

   A   **B**   **C**   **D**   **N**

13. my leg. Although I wasn't seriously hurt, it will leave a massive briuse on my shin!

   A   **B**   **C**   **D**   **N**

END OF TEST

/ 18

That's another batch of tests completed. Now let's practise your **word skills**.

Ridiculous Riddles

The answer to each of the riddles below is a letter.
The letters will spell out a hidden five-letter word.

My first is in bicker, but not in trickier.

My second is in barter, but not in bitter.

My third is in eleven but not in lever.

My fourth is in rejoice but not in choicer.

My fifth is in royal but not in yearly.

I am a _ _ _ _ _.

My first is in lemon, but not in golden.

My second is in piglet, but not in plotting.

My third is in blonde but not in bonded.

My fourth is in older but not in leader.

My fifth is in nugget but not in gutter.

I am a _ _ _ _ _.

Wall of the Words

Use the clues given to fill in the word wall. Each word uses the same
letters as the word before, with one letter either added or taken away.
The letters don't have to be in the same order as the word before, though.

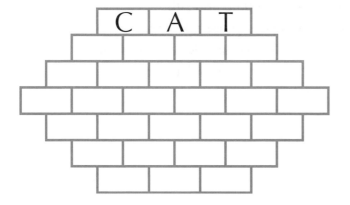

a feline family pet

a vehicle pulled by a horse

to provide food and drink

a loud, unpleasant noise

to make a squeaking sound

a tool used for tidying leaves

the ship built by Noah

You have **10 minutes** to do this test. Work as quickly and accurately as you can.

Read this poem carefully and answer the questions that follow.

O Captain! My Captain!

O Captain! my Captain! our fearful trip is done;
The ship has weathered every rack*, the prize we sought is won;
The port is near, the bells I hear, the people all exulting*,
While follow eyes the steady keel*, the vessel grim and daring:
5   But O heart! heart! heart!
         O the bleeding drops of red,
            Where on the deck my Captain lies,
             Fallen cold and dead.

O Captain! my Captain! rise up and hear the bells;
10 Rise up — for you the flag is flung — for you the bugle trills;
For you bouquets and ribboned wreaths — for you the shores a-crowding;
For you they call, the swaying mass, their eager faces turning;
      Here Captain! dear father!
        This arm beneath your head;
15   It is some dream that on the deck,
          You've fallen cold and dead.

My Captain does not answer, his lips are pale and still;
My father does not feel my arm, he has no pulse nor will;
The ship is anchored safe and sound, its voyage closed and done;
20 From fearful trip, the victor ship, comes in with object won;
      Exult, O shores, and ring, O bells!
        But I, with mournful tread,
          Walk the deck my Captain lies,
            Fallen cold and dead.

Walt Whitman

* rack — *storm*
*to exult — *to rejoice or be delighted*
*keel — *the underside of a ship*

70

1. Which of these words is closest in meaning to "sought" (line 2)?
    Tick the box next to the correct answer.

    A   Squandered   ☐

    B   Appreciated   ☐

    C   Exchanged   ☐

    D   Pursued   ☐

2. Which of following best describes the voyage of the ship?
    Tick the box next to the correct answer.

    A   An unsuccessful voyage fraught with difficulty   ☐

    B   A successful, straightforward voyage   ☐

    C   A successful voyage that was challenging   ☐

    D   An unsuccessful but enjoyable voyage   ☐

3. "While follow eyes the steady keel" (line 4).
    Which word in this phrase is an adjective?

    _____

4. "But O heart! heart! heart!" (line 5).
    What is this sentence an example of? Tick the box next to the correct answer.

    A   Metaphor   ☐

    B   Repetition   ☐

    C   Personification   ☐

    D   Onomatopoeia   ☐

TURN OVER ➡

5. Look at lines 11-12. Give one way that the crowd celebrate the returning ship.

    _____

    _____

6. Which of the following best describes how the narrator feels in the second verse?
    Tick the box next to the correct answer.

    A   He is inconsolable about the Captain's death.   ☐

    B   He is worried how the crowd will react to the Captain's death.   ☐

    C   He is in disbelief about the Captain's death.   ☐

    D   He is furious that someone has murdered the Captain.   ☐

7. What relationship do you think the narrator has with the Captain?

    _____

8. Give another word or phrase that means the same as
    "victor" (line 20) as it is used in the text.

    _____

9. Which of these statements is true? Tick the box next to the correct answer.

    A   The ship cannot anchor without the Captain.   ☐

    B   The Captain's body is thrown overboard.   ☐

    C   The crowd mourns the fallen Captain.   ☐

    D   It is not clear from the poem how the Captain died.   ☐

END OF TEST

/ 9

Test 26: Proofreading

You have **10 minutes** to do this test. Work as quickly and accurately as you can.

For each numbered line, choose the word, or group of words,
which completes the passage correctly. The passage needs to make
sense and be written in correct English. Circle the correct letter.

1. Catherine had **broke** **break** **broken** **breaks** **breaked** her grandmother's
         A   B   C   D   E

2. valuable vase and was frantically **tried** **trying** **trieing** **try** **tries** to glue it back
                                          A   B   C   D   E

3. together. She **wasn't** **shan't** **couldn't** **shouldn't** **isn't** manage to do it, so she
                       A   B   C   D   E

4. sneaked out to try to **finds** **find** **finding** **found** **founder** a cheap replacement.
                              A   B   C   D   E

This passage has some punctuation mistakes.
Write the passage out again with the correct punctuation.

5.   "Would you like a drink? william asked."
      "please could, I have a lemonade? Sayeeda replied.

_____

_____

_____

TURN OVER ➡

This passage contains some spelling mistakes. Each numbered line has either one mistake or no mistake. For each line, work out which group of words contains a mistake, and circle the correct letter. Circle N if there is no mistake.

6. Beijul began the water fight by fireing the first water balloon at David. It was
   A   **B**   **C**   **D**   **N**

7. definitely a mistake to make an enemy out of David — he was possitioned near to
   A   **B**   **C**   **D**   **N**

8. the wall and had easy access to the hosepipe. Suprisingly, David marched to the
   A   **B**   **C**   **D**   **N**

9. paddling pool and grabbed a sponge, squeazing it slowly onto Beijul's hair.
   A   **B**   **C**   **D**   **N**

10. Beijul heard his mum come in through the front door and suggested they soke
    A   **B**   **C**   **D**   **N**

11. her with the hose. When she obliviously stepped out into the garden, they both
    A   **B**   **C**   **D**   **N**

12. drenched her with water. As she screamed, they realised how thoughtles they'd
    A   **B**   **C**   **D**   **N**

13. been. She was carrying the burgers that they were going to barbicue for dinner.
    A   **B**   **C**   **D**   **N**

END OF TEST

/ 18

You have **10 minutes** to do this test. Work as quickly and accurately as you can.

Read this passage carefully and answer the questions that follow.

Bees

Bees might be small creatures, but they are amongst the most important because they play an essential role in producing the food we eat. In fact, we might not be able to survive without them.

When you see these diligent little insects flitting from flower to flower, they are not
5   only collecting nectar for their own food, but they are also inadvertently helping the plants to reproduce. While they use their long tongues to collect nectar from inside the flowers, pollen is collected on their legs. The bees dart among the nearby flora and fauna*, transferring pollen to the plants and allowing them to pollinate — that is, to produce seeds. This helps to grow more of the fruit and vegetables that we eat.
10 Despite many crops having alternative sources of pollination, such as the wind or birds, it's thought that in a world without bees, supermarkets would only be able to stock around half the fruit and vegetable products normally available.

Of course, bees also produce food for us directly. Honeybees have been farmed by humans for centuries. They produce honey by collecting nectar from flowers, bringing
15 it back to a hive and allowing the water from the nectar to evaporate, making thick and gloopy honey. Honeybees also create wax, which is used to produce candles, cosmetics and furniture polish, amongst other things.

Sadly, bee numbers are dwindling and this is cause for great concern among both farmers and environmentalists. No one is exactly sure why bees are dying out, but
20 several theories have been proposed. For example, many farmers put chemicals on their crops to try to kill insects that might eat them, and these chemicals are often also harmful for bees. Disease has also killed many honeybees living in hives, and many bee habitats have been destroyed to build farms and houses.

* flora and fauna — *plants and animals*

TURN OVER ➡

1. "we might not be able to survive without them" (lines 2-3). What type of word is "without" as it is used in this phrase? Tick the box next to the correct answer.

   A   Adverb   ☐

   B   Adjective   ☐

   C   Preposition   ☐

   D   Verb   ☐

2. Find a word from the text that means the same as 'hard-working'.

   _____

3. "flitting from flower to flower" (line 4). Which technique is this an example of?

   _____

4. Why do bees need to collect nectar from flowers?

   _____

5. According to the text, why are bees so important for humans?
   Tick the box next to the correct answer.

   A   They collect nectar from a variety of flowers.   ☐

   B   They help fruit and vegetables grow.   ☐

   C   They add to the diversity of wildlife.   ☐

   D   They help stop climate change.   ☐

6. According to the text, which of the following statements is false?
   Tick the box next to the correct answer.

   A   Honey has been consumed by humans for hundreds of years.   ☐

   B   Honeybee wax can be used to make candles.   ☐

   C   Honey is made from pollen.   ☐

   D   Honey is made in a hive.   ☐

7. Find a word or phrase that tells you how the author feels about the decline in bees.

   _____

8. Give another word or phrase that means the same as
   "dwindling" (line 18) as it is used in the text.

   _____

9. Which of the following is not mentioned as a reason for the lack of bees?
   Tick the box next to the correct answer.

   A   Disease is spreading among honeybees.   ☐

   B   Their habitats are being destroyed.   ☐

   C   Humans are eating too much honey.   ☐

   D   Chemicals on plants are killing bees.   ☐

END OF TEST

/ 9

No doubt you're ready for a couple of puzzles. These ones test your **word-type** skills.

Wacky Wordsearch

There are six adjectives hidden in the wordsearch. The nouns below give you a clue what to look for.

Nouns:	
activity	scene
fear	creation
boredom	envy

```
L A G F P I K A J
B O R I N G E C R
S E S W E N A I D
A C J N H B O N S
C R E A T I V E A
T W U L E H N C K
I E N V I O U S N
V T P A D S Y C A
E G F E A R F U L
```

Word Ladder

Make your way down the word ladder by changing one letter each time. Use the clues to help you fill in the missing words.

sink	
	feeling ill
	a large bag
	the rear
	land next to a river
	the noise a dog makes
barn	

You have **10 minutes** to do this test. Work as quickly and accurately as you can.

Read this passage carefully and answer the questions that follow.

An adapted extract from 'The Dream Woman'

We pass through the open arched doorway, and find no one to welcome us. We advance into the stable yard and I help my wife to dismount. No bell to ring. Nobody answers when I call. I stand helpless, with the bridles of the horses in my hand. My wife saunters gracefully down the length of the yard, opens every door as she passes
5 it, and peeps in. On my side, I have just recovered my breath; I am on the point of shouting for the hostler* for the third and last time, when I hear my wife suddenly call to me:

"Percy! Come here!"

Her voice is eager and agitated. She has opened one last door at the end of the
10 yard, and has jumped back from some sight which has suddenly met her view. I hitch the horses' bridles on a rusty nail in the wall near me, and join her. She is as pale as milk, and catches me nervously by the arm.

"Good heavens!" she cries, "Look at that!"

I look — and what do I see? I see a dingy little stable, containing two stalls. In one
15 stall a horse is munching his corn. In the other a man is lying asleep on the hay.

A worn, withered, woebegone* man dressed as a hostler. His hollow wrinkled cheeks, his scanty grizzled hair, his dry yellow skin, tell their own tale of past sorrow or suffering. There is an ominous frown on his eyebrows — there is a painful nervous contraction on the side of his mouth. I hear him breathing irregularly when I first look
20 in; he shudders and sighs in his sleep. It is not a pleasant sight to see, and I turn round instinctively to the bright sunlight in the yard.

Wilkie Collins

* hostler — *a person who looks after horses*
* woebegone — *looking sad or miserable*

TURN OVER ➡

1. Write down a word or phrase from the text which suggests that Percy's wife moves elegantly.

_____

2. Why do you think Percy's wife opens "every door as she passes it, and peeps in" (lines 4-5)? Tick the box next to the correct answer.

   A   She is nosy. ☐

   B   She is looking for her horse. ☐

   C   She is looking for someone. ☐

   D   She is trying to find her way out of the yard. ☐

3. How many times does Percy shout for the hostler?

_____

4. How does Percy's wife feel when she finds the hostler? Tick the box next to the correct answer.

   A   Disappointed and annoyed ☐

   B   Happy and relieved ☐

   C   Disgusted and horrified ☐

   D   Surprised and anxious ☐

5. Give another word or phrase that means the same as "hitch" (line 10) as it is used in the text.

_____

       80

6. "She is as pale as milk" (lines 11-12). What is this phrase an example of?

_____

7. Lines 17-18 state that the hostler's physical features "tell their own tale of past sorrow or suffering". What does this mean? Tick the box next to the correct answer.

   A   He is in pain.   ☐

   B   He looks old.   ☐

   C   He has had a tough life.   ☐

   D   He is lazy.   ☐

8. "there is a painful nervous contraction" (lines 18-19).
    Which word in this phrase is a noun?

_____

9. Why does Percy "turn round instinctively to the bright sunlight in the yard" (lines 20-21)? Tick the box next to the correct answer.

   A   The yard looks beautiful in the sunlight.   ☐

   B   The stables smell bad and he needs fresh air.   ☐

   C   He doesn't want to look at the hostler any more.   ☐

   D   His wife has called him from the yard.   ☐

END OF TEST

/ 9

You have **10 minutes** to do this test. Work as quickly and accurately as you can.

This passage contains some spelling mistakes.
Write the passage out again with the correct spellings.

1.   Naomi's parcel had been deliverred next door by mistake and she wanted her dad
     to go and ask for it — she was reluctent to go by herself. Naomi tried to persuede
     her dad, but he refused. Apperently going by herself was 'character-bilding'.

     _____

     _____

     _____

     _____

This passage has some punctuation mistakes.
Write the passage out again with the correct punctuation.

2.   Ahmed was going to corfu (in Greece at the Weekend. As he packed he was
     worried that, his suitcase wasn't big enough.

     _____

     _____

     _____

82

3. Often inaccurately referred to **by as after with of** the Norfolk Broads, the
    A B   C   D   E

4. Broads are a series of rivers and lakes **where which who what whom** cover
          A   B   C   D   E

5. areas of both Norfolk and Suffolk. They **were is was will be are** man-made
          A   B   C   D   E

6. waterways and today are **using use useless used useful** by sailors, who
          A   B   C   D   E

7. navigate **around under above off near** the Broads on small yachts.
        A   B   C   D   E

8. Windmills scatter the area and **towering tower towers towered toward**
          A   B   C   D   E

9. over the famously flat, rural landscape. The rivers **flews flows flowed flow flew**
          A   B   C   D   E

10. **after with through across atop** many beautiful small towns and villages,
    A   B   C   D   E

    as well as the cathedral city of Norwich, before finally reaching the Broads.

END OF TEST

/ 18

Test 29

You have **10 minutes** to do this test. Work as quickly and accurately as you can.

> Read this passage carefully and answer the questions that follow.

Morocco

Bustling mazes of tiny winding alleyways lined with noisy market stalls, the souks are one of the principal attractions of Marrakesh, in southern Morocco. Locals and tourists alike flock to these markets to haggle for dried fruits, colourful spices, leather pouffes*, Berber carpets and a whole host of other North African goods. This area
5   is called the "medina" and most of its streets are far too narrow to allow cars to pass through.

The beating heart of the medina is the Jemaa el-Fnaa, a square of food stalls and restaurants in the centre of the city that comes alive at night with a wide array of performers. Snake charmers enchant cobras with flutes, while traditional storytellers
10   enthral onlookers with their tales. Overlooking the square is the Koutoubia mosque, perhaps Marrakesh's most iconic building. It towers over the area thanks to a law preventing any buildings of a similar height from being built.

If you travel southeast from Marrakesh, through a narrow mountain pass, you arrive at the city of Ouarzazate. Known as 'the gateway to the Sahara', the city is just north
15   of the desert. It contains many kasbahs (or fortresses) and is a popular film-making location due to its distinctive surroundings.

Any trip to Morocco would not be complete without tasting some of its culinary specialities. Perhaps the most famous of these is tagine: a slow-cooked stew often flavoured with fruit such as dates or dried apricots. Couscous is another food widely
20   eaten in Morocco — it is commonly flavoured with a spice mix known as 'ras el-hanout' and eaten with meat and vegetables. If a Moroccan offers you some 'atai', make sure to say yes. It's a hot green tea mixed with mint and sugar. It plays an important ceremonial role and it's considered rude in Morocco to refuse tea.

* pouffes — *cushioned footstools (can also be used as seating)*

Answer these questions about the text. You can refer back to the text if you need to.

1. What does the word "souks" (line 1) refer to? Tick the box next to the correct answer.

    A   Attractions   ☐

    B   Markets   ☐

    C   Alleyways   ☐

    D   Stalls   ☐

2. "Locals and tourists alike flock to these markets" (lines 2-3).
   Which word is a verb? Tick the box next to the correct answer.

    A   flock   ☐

    B   tourists   ☐

    C   markets   ☐

    D   locals   ☐

3. Why do you think the Jemaa el-Fnaa is called the "beating heart of the medina" (line 7)?

   _____

   _____

4. Give another word or phrase that means the same as "enthral" (line 10) as it is used in the text.

   _____

5. Why do you think the Koutoubia mosque "towers" (line 11) over the medina?

   _____

TURN OVER ➡

Test 30

6. Explain in your own words why Ouarzazate is "a popular film-making location" (lines 15-16).

_____

_____

7. Explain in your own words what the phrase "culinary specialities" (lines 17-18) means.

_____

8. Which of the following statements about Moroccan food is true? Tick the box next to the correct answer.

   A   Most Moroccans don't eat meat. ☐

   B   Ras el-hanout is a typical Moroccan meal. ☐

   C   Fruit is used in savoury dishes in Morocco. ☐

   D   Tagine is similar to a soup. ☐

9. According to the text, why should you accept if a Moroccan offers you "atai" (line 21)? Tick the box next to the correct answer.

   A   It's bad luck to refuse. ☐

   B   Atai is a delicious delicacy. ☐

   C   Atai is cooling and refreshing. ☐

   D   It is impolite to refuse. ☐

END OF TEST

/ 9

Puzzles 10

Time for a break! Test your **grammar** and **word-making** skills with these puzzles.

Treasure and Tenses

Rohan has found a mysterious scroll that will lead him to some lost treasure, but his clues have some mistakes in them. Underline the incorrect verbs in the clues and write the correct form of the verb on the line beside it.

I had spend years searching for the treasure, but to no avail. _____

Then I met Peggy the Pirate, who claimed to knew its location. _____

I were given these instructions: _____

"Started in the shadow of the old ghost ship. _____

Turn right and goes straight into the jungle. _____

Be sure to walked quickly, for there are crocodiles. _____

You will found the treasure in a hidden grove." _____

That is all I can telling you. Good luck, matey... _____

Compound Creations

For each group of words below, find a word that can be added to the front or the end of each word to make four new words. The first one has been done for you.

1)   life ?   mean ?   any ?   day ?   <u>t i m e</u>

2)   ? drop   ? bone   ? stage   ? hand   _ _ _ _

3)   drive ?   rail ?   any ?   walk ?   _ _ _

4)   ? stream   ? load   ? stairs   ? hill   _ _

You have **10 minutes** to do this test. Work as quickly and accurately as you can.

> For each numbered line, choose the word, or group of words, which completes the passage correctly. The passage needs to make sense and be written in correct English. Circle the correct letter.

Dear Maureen,

1. Colin and I **am are is was will be** having a wonderful time in Blackpool. The
                 A   B   C   D   E

2. weather has been atrocious, but we're **taking talking having making spending**
                                        A   B   C   D   E

3. the most of it anyway. Colin wanted to **went going gone goes go** for a ride on
                                       A   B   C   D E

4. a donkey, **despite due to but and instead** he's too big for that.
               A   B   C   D   E

Wish you were here, Alison x

> This passage has some punctuation mistakes.
> Write the passage out again with the correct punctuation.

5. Keen to impress Jamal has been trying to learn some french before next Summer.
Hes going to stay with his penpal, Sid in Marseille on Frances' Mediterranean coast.

_____

_____

_____

This passage contains some spelling mistakes. Each numbered line has either one mistake or no mistake. For each line, work out which group of words contains a mistake, and circle the correct letter. Circle N if there is no mistake.

6. Despite Toni's protests, the steward was unwavering. He refused to let her into the

        A   B   C   D   N

7. theme park without a ticket. Of course, this would be quite understandible, but Toni

        A   B   C   D   N

8. had already been admitted to the park, and she had accidentally left without her

        A   B   C   D   N

9. ticket when she went to meet her brother. She attempted to negotiate with him,

        A   B   C   D   N

10. saying if he accompanied her into the park, she could find her ticket and proove

        A   B   C   D   N

11. that she was allowed to be there. She pleaded and aregued, but he was completely

        A   B   C   D   N

12. uninterested. Toni had never met someone so lacking in compasion before. When

        A   B   C   D   N

13. he was distracted, she sneeked past him and sprinted gleefully into the theme park.

        A   B   C   D   N

END OF TEST

/ 18

You have **10 minutes** to do this test. Work as quickly and accurately as you can.

Read this passage carefully and answer the questions that follow.

Liquid Gold

Drake reached into his satchel for the seventeenth time that morning. He rifled through the pouch's contents, his hand a slithering eel burrowing into ocean sand. He fingered a hessian* sack and palmed a handful of gold coins within it. He contemplated how, if he were back in England, he could live like a king and have
5   hundreds of gallons of fresh, crystal clear spring water brought to him.

"I'd happily exchange all the gold I found in the cave for a gulp of water," Drake mused to himself, harking back to the treasure trove he had found the previous evening. After convincing himself that the satchel didn't bear the waterskin*, he withdrew his arm dejectedly.

10   "Argh!" he winced, and noticed a stream of red trickle down his wrist. He'd nicked himself on the gold-hilted knife that he'd found in the hoard of riches. He wondered if it had been worthwhile to replace his last waterskin for the ornamental dagger, and simultaneously wondered if the entire expedition had been worth it at all.

For the next few hours, the beating sun lashed his body remorselessly. By this time,
15   he was parched and his tongue begged for a drop of liquid gold. The Sahara desert was vast and intimidating. Its sprawling, abandoned plains were a far cry from the bustling markets of Cairo, which had been Drake's first port of call. Without a map or compass, Drake felt utterly helpless and he fell to his knees with a rasping sigh.

Then, Drake spotted something. The intense heat and glare of the sun had blurred
20   the distant shape, but there was no doubt in his mind of what he saw: an oasis*. He arose gleefully and bounded towards the desert haven, leaving his newfound wealth behind. Palm trees enveloped a sparkling spring, into which Drake dived head first, guzzling water as if he were inhaling air.

* hessian — *a strong fabric*
* waterskin — *a small pouch used to carry water*
* oasis — *a fertile area in the desert*

1. Why do you think Drake had searched the satchel for water sixteen times already?

    _____

2. "his hand a slithering eel burrowing into ocean sand" (line 2).
    What is this phrase an example of? Tick the box next to the correct answer.

    A   Simile   ☐

    B   Personification   ☐

    C   Metaphor   ☐

    D   Alliteration   ☐

3. Which of the following statements is true? Tick the box next to the correct answer.

    A   Drake had found the treasure the week before.   ☐

    B   Drake was a monarch from England.   ☐

    C   His satchel contained only a sack and some coins.   ☐

    D   Drake had found the treasure in a cave.   ☐

4. "he withdrew his arm dejectedly" (line 9). Which of these words is a verb?
    Tick the box next to the correct answer.

    A   he   ☐

    B   withdrew   ☐

    C   arm   ☐

    D   dejectedly   ☐

TURN OVER ➡

5. Give another word or phrase that means the same as "simultaneously" (line 13).

_____

6. Find a word or phrase from the text that means the same as 'brutally'.

_____

7. Why do you think water is referred to as "liquid gold" (line 15)?

_____

_____

8. Which of these isn't given as a reason why Drake didn't notice the oasis straightaway?

    A   The oasis was far away.   ☐

    B   The brightness of the sun made the oasis hard to see.   ☐

    C   The oasis was concealed by a sand dune.   ☐

    D   The heat had blurred the oasis from view.   ☐

9. Which of the following words best describes how Drake drinks from the spring?

    A   Desperately   ☐

    B   Carefully   ☐

    C   Angrily   ☐

    D   Joyously   ☐

END OF TEST

/ 9

You have **10 minutes** to do this test. Work as quickly and accurately as you can.

> For each numbered line, choose the word, or group of words,
> which completes the passage correctly. The passage needs to make
> sense and be written in correct English. Circle the correct letter.

1. The best two things about my local area **are** **is** **will be** **won't** **was** the cinema
                     A   B   C   D   E

2. and the swimming pool. I'm a very **enjoyable** **thrilled** **keen** **adore** **favourite**
                      A   B   C   D   E

3. swimmer, so it means I can go for a **swum** **swim** **swimming** **swam** **swimmed**
                      A   B   C   D   E

4. three times a week. It's in easy walking **distance** **length** **away** **far** **path** too.
                      A   B   C   D   E

> This passage contains some spelling mistakes.
> Write the passage out again with the correct spellings.

5. The solider was throughly soaked and every mussle in his body ached. The
    appalling weather and the tough, mountainous enviroment had been a hinderance
    and he was worried that he wouldn't complete the training exersise quickly enough.

    _____

    _____

    _____

    _____

TURN OVER ➡

       93

This passage contains some punctuation mistakes. Each numbered line has either one mistake or no mistake. For each line, work out which group of words contains a mistake, and circle the correct letter. Circle N if there is no mistake.

6. The green anaconda is one of the worlds longest snakes. These large, fearsome

       A   B   C   D   N

7. predators live in the swamps and marshes of south America. Because of their

       A   B   C   D   N

8. enormous size they find it much easier to travel through the water than on land.

       A   B   C   D   N

9. green anacondas are not venomous, so they rely on strangling their prey to kill it.

       A   B   C   D   N

10. They mostly eat small animals (such as fish and birds, but they sometimes attack

       A   B   C   D   N

11. larger animals (such as tapirs). When they try to eat larger prey anacondas can

       A   B   C   D   N

12. unhinge their jaws and swallow the animals whole. So watch out if you're in the

       A   B   C   D   N

13. Amazon and spot two eyes, poking out of the river — it could be an anaconda.

       A   B   C   D   N

END OF TEST

/ 18

F6XP2F1